The Parents' Handbook to the 7+ Entrance Exams
An Indispensable Guide

By Ilana King

Contents:

Why follow my guidance? 1
About the exams 2
How to get the most from this book 2
Starting early 3
The importance of vocabulary 5
Reading Comprehension 7
Writing Composition 15
Dictation 23
Maths 27
Verbal Reasoning 35
Non-Verbal Reasoning 43
Exam techniques 49
Keeping Track of Progress 55
Staying positive 71
Interview and assessment day preparation 75
Recommended reading list 79
Further information and guidance 80
Practise English exam 81
Practise Maths exam 95
Practise Reasoning exam 105

Why follow my guidance?

Most schools will tell you that you do not need to do any special preparation with your child for entrance exams. Over many years of supporting parents and children in their preparation for entry into some of London's top preparatory schools, it has become clear to me that this is an unbalanced view.

Imagine being asked to cook a completely unfamiliar dish with no recipe to follow! You may know how to cook. You may even be familiar with some of the ingredients, but if you have not made the dish before you will certainly need a step by step guide on how to put them together.

As an educator with over twenty five years of experience, and a specialist in 7+ entrance exams, I can provide these steps for you. Over the years, I have used my extensive knowledge of the exam process to successfully help parents understand how to inspire their children to achieve excellence and reach success in these exams.

What is the 7+ exam?

This book has been designed as a handbook to help you navigate the pathway of preparing your child for the 7+ school entrance exams. The 7+ assessment is a competitive selection process used by an increasing number of top schools in London and beyond for entry into Year 3. The 7+ exam is taken part way through year two.

Although each school has a different exam, they all primarily test Maths and English. An increasing number of schools now also include a Reasoning paper containing either Verbal or Non-Verbal Reasoning, or both. The tests are usually in a written format but there can be listening sections, testing mental arithmetic, spelling, memory and dictation.

How to get the most from this book

Preparing your child for the 7+ exam can feel like an insurmountable pathway to navigate. This book has been designed as a guide to help you navigate this pathway, breaking down each element of the exam and giving you clear guidance each step of the way. Included from page 68 are attainment target charts for you to keep track of how your child is progressing. The final section of the book has full practice exams for the period just before the assessments take place.

Starting early

Parents often ask me when is the best time to begin preparation. It is never too early to begin. As you read about each element of the assessment, you will see that you can work on the foundation skills from up to two years before the exam. The rate at which your child will need to progress will be reduced by an early start, putting less pressure on everyone. If you are coming to this guide later in the process, don't panic! As you work through each section, you may well discover that your child has already reached the attainment levels in many areas and you can focus on the sections where further progress needs to be made.

The Importance of Vocabulary

Vocabulary is integral to all areas of the 7+ entrance exams. It is tested explicitly in both the English and Verbal Reasoning portions of the exams, as well as implicitly throughout reading comprehension, writing composition and maths word problems.

Where is vocabulary knowledge tested on the exams?

- **Reading comprehension:** To fully understand the text, your child will need to know the vocabulary within it. In addition, there are often specific questions asking students to define a word from the text or to identify a synonym for that word.
- **Composition:** Schools are looking for children who show a mature and varied use of vocabulary in their writing.
- **Verbal Reasoning:** This section of the exam will contain exercises in which your child will need to identify words with similar meaning, opposite meanings, as well as finding links between groups of words.
- **Maths:** Word problems make up a significant portion of the maths section of the 7+ exam and often are worth the most points. To be able to decipher what maths they need to do, your child will need to be able to read and understand the question, including the maths vocabulary within it.

Ideally, vocabulary should be developed through activities beginning when children are pre-verbal. It then continues to grow throughout their early years and into their school years. If, however, you feel that your child's vocabulary is an area of weakness and is hindering their progress in some or all areas of the exam preparation, it is not too late to make progress.

Key targeted activities for vocabulary:

- **Reading:** Children should be reading high-quality literature. Encourage your child to read to themselves, but also take time to read to them. At times, when this is not possible, audio books are an excellent alternative.

- **Writing:** New vocabulary becomes more embedded with use. Your child should be encouraged to use new words in their writing compositions.

- Don't "dumb down" conversations with your child. Use new vocabulary and discuss words that are unfamiliar to them.

- Board games, such as Junior Scrabble, Bananagram and Hangman, as well as verbal games such as "I Spy" and Guess the Word are all fun ways of extending vocabulary.

What is it?

Reading comprehension refers to the understanding and interpretation of what is read. In answering comprehension questions, children are being tested on their ability to decode what they read and make connections between what they have read and what they already know.

How is it tested?

Reading comprehension passages can vary in difficulty and genre quite significantly across exams. The question types can be multiple choice, long answer (where full sentences are required) or a combination of both. However, the underlying skills being tested remain the same, regardless of the variations.

What are the key skills my child needs to learn?

- Read fluently
- Summarise what they have read
- Answer literal questions
- Draw inferences about the text
- Understand and define words in context
- Identify and comment on language that contributes to meaning
- Make predictions

First Steps:

Reading comprehension begins with reading aloud to an adult and discussing the text. This important stage is often missed in 7+ preparation, with children being given written questions to answer as the first step. The key skills listed on the previous page can all be gently introduced through verbal discussion while reading together, an enjoyable activity for your child that will not feel like work! Use the recommended book list on page 67 to choose enjoyable and challenging books to share with your child.

Moving on:

When your child can read fluently and is comfortable with discussing what they have read, it is time to introduce written questions. Text passages should be simple and ask only **literal** questions. These are questions in which the answer is stated explicitly in the text. These questions only require your child to use their recall of the text to answer. Your child can refer back to the text to find the answer easily. They must then just put the answer in a full sentence to respond. There are many commercially produced comprehension books containing short passages that can be used at this stage of the process.

Once your child is able to competently answer literal questions about a passage, it is time to move on to **inference** questions. Inference questions do not have a direct and explicit answer in the text. They require your child to look for clues in the text and use these clues to help them answer the questions. Sometimes they refer to a specific part of the text, and sometimes they will call for your child to think about the text as a whole.

Inference questions often begin with "why" and ask your child to make a link between an action or emotion and its cause. These questions are the most challenging for children preparing for the 7+ exams and will require the most practice. Your child will need to make connections between the descriptive language used in the passage (for example: "trembling" to describe a person's body language) and what it tells them about what is happening. Additionally, they will need to think about cause and effect (why did something happen).

Helpful tips:

- Written answers can feel like a chore if done too often. The same comprehension skills can be practised when answers are given aloud, so mix it up and give your child a combination of ways to respond.

- Children often find questions that link body language clues to emotion the most tricky to answer. Play guessing games in which you take turns expressing an emotion through body language only.

- When reading to your child, ask them "why" questions. You can stop at the end of a chapter or even a page and discuss what you have read.

- Challenge your child to ask *you* a comprehension question about a book you are reading together. By coming up with a question and answer themselves, your child will think more deeply about the text while still having fun!

Example:

Below is a typical comprehension passage. Following the passage are questions and answers of the various types that test the key skills that have been discussed in the previous section.

Once upon a time there were four little Rabbits, and their names were Flopsy, Mopsy, Cotton-tail, and Peter. They lived with their Mother in a sand-bank, underneath the root of a very big fir-tree. "Now, my dears," said old Mrs. Rabbit one morning, "you may go into the fields or down the lane, but don't go into Mr. McGregor's garden. "Your Father had an accident there; he was put in a pie by Mrs. McGregor. "Now run along, and don't get into mischief. I am going out."

Then old Mrs. Rabbit took a basket and her umbrella, and went through the wood to the baker's. She bought a loaf of brown bread and five currant buns. Flopsy, Mopsy and Cotton-tail, who were good little bunnies, went down the lane to gather blackberries; but Peter, who was very naughty, ran straight away to Mr. McGregor's garden, and squeezed under the gate!

First he ate some lettuce and some French beans; and then he ate some radishes; and then, feeling rather sick, he went to look for some parsley. But round the end of a cucumber frame, whom should he meet but Mr. McGregor! Mr. McGregor was on his hands and knees planting out young cabbages, but he jumped up and ran

11

after Peter, waving a rake and calling out, "Stop thief!" Peter was most dreadfully frightened; he rushed all over the garden, for he had forgotten the way back to the gate. He lost one of his shoes among the cabbages, and the other shoe amongst the potatoes.

After losing them, he ran on four legs and went faster, so that I think he might have got away altogether if he had not unfortunately run into a gooseberry net, and got caught by the large buttons on his jacket. It was a blue jacket with brass buttons, quite new. Peter gave himself up for lost, and shed big tears; but his sobs were overheard by some friendly sparrows, who flew to him in great excitement, and implored him to exert himself.

Mr. McGregor came up with a sieve, which he intended to pop upon the top of Peter; but Peter wriggled out just in time, leaving his jacket behind him, and rushed into the tool-shed, and jumped into a can. It would have been a beautiful thing to hide in, if it had not had so much water in it.

Taken from "The Tale of Peter the Rabbit" by Beatrix Potter

Where did the rabbits live?

This is a literal question. The answer can be found explicitly in the text in the first section.

Answer:
The rabbits lived in a sand-bank, underneath the root of a very big fir-tree.

Why did Mr McGregor run after Peter?

This is an inference question. It does not explicitly state in the text why he did this. Your child must look at what preceded this action, and make the connection between that and why Mr McGregor might run after Peter.

Answer:
Mr McGregor ran after Peter because Peter had stolen his vegetables and Mr McGregor was angry at him.

What does this sentence tell us about how Peter was feeling 'Peter gave himself up for lost, and shed big tears...'?

Answer:

Peter was feeling very upset about not being able to escape from Mr McGregor as he was crying.

What does the phrase "implored him to exert himself" mean?

This question tests vocabulary knowledge and the ability to explain a difficult phrase.

Answer:

This phrase means that the sparrows wanted Peter to try harder.

What do you think happened to Peter after he jumped into the watering can?

This is a question that is asking your child to predict what happens next. While it does ask them to use their imagination, they must also use the information that has been given in the text already. A response full of imagination but not based on the text will not be given marks.

(For example: *I think that a monster appeared and took Peter and the watering can to his cave.*)

Answer:

I think that Peter had to get out of the can as it was too wet and Mr McGregor caught him and told him off for stealing his vegetables.

What is it?

Writing tasks vary widely across exams, although the focus will usually be on story writing. Children have a difficult task of still needing to focus on basic skills such as handwriting, spelling and grammar while thinking about the content of their writing.

How is it tested?

For many schools, the composition task is part of the first stage written assessment process. However, for some schools, composition does not form part of the first stage exam and is tested during the second stage assessment day. In both instances, children are usually given a prompt and asked to write for a set amount of time. The prompt can take many different forms including:

- a story title
- a picture
- multiple pictures for elements of the story (a character, a setting and an object for instance)
- a "continue the story" task using either the comprehension or a short video.

What are the key skills my child needs to learn?

- Creating and sustaining an imaginative narrative with a beginning, middle and end

- Writing using mature and varied vocabulary, including complex sentence structure and literary techniques

- Clear and neat presentation including accurate spelling and grammar

First Steps:

Although composition is a written skill, it should begin verbally. Start by asking your child to tell you a story. You can use a picture as a prompt, or give them a specific situation around which to create their narrative. Your child should be able to tell you a story that has a clear beginning, middle and end.

If they are struggling with this, you can model how to do it by telling them a story first. It can be fun to take turns with a story, with each of you telling one part and handing over to the other. Challenge your child to surprise you with how they end the story!

16

Once your child is comfortably telling you stories verbally, it is time to begin to write them down. Initially, children find it challenging to write a whole story on paper, as there is so much for them to remember to do.

You can take small steps towards a whole written story by asking them to first write the beginning paragraph and then dictate the rest for you to write down. Build up slowly with your child writing more and more of the story themselves.

In this step, the focus should be on the content of the story and not the vocabulary or sentence structure. The aim is for your child to write a three paragraph story that is imaginative and has narrative flow. It should have:

- a clear beginning in which the character/s and setting are introduced with some description

- a middle in which the character/s encounter an exciting problem

- an ending in which the problem is resolved and the character/s reflects on what has happened.

Next steps:

If your child is able to write a three paragraph story that flows from a beginning to an end and relates back to the prompt given, it is time to focus on the language within the story. Begin by using a story your child has already written. Ask them to think about ways in which it can be improved:

- adding adjectives and description

- extending simple sentences by adding clauses

- ensuring that sentences have varied openings and structure.

Once your child understands how to improve stories they have already written, they can begin to write from scratch and focus on the language they are using. Begin with writing only one part of the story (beginnings, middles or ends) before moving on to writing entire stories.

Helpful tips:

- Story telling does not need to be confined to formal preparation sessions. Telling stories on walks, in the car, in the garden, or anytime you are out and about will help your child develop the skills to construct a narrative. Use what you see around you, or a situation you are in, as a prompt.

- Play word games to develop descriptive language. Choose an object in sight and describe it using only adjectives without naming the object. Can they guess what it is? Take turns. Choose a boring adjective and compete over who can come up with the most interesting synonym.

- Story dice are a fun way to make story telling into a game. The pictures on these dice act as prompts in the story-telling process and by taking turns rolling and adding to the story, the results can sometimes be hilarious!

- Most importantly, story writing should be fun! By using a variety of approaches rather than just formal writing session, your child can develop a love of story-telling.

Example:

This story was written by a student preparing for the 7+ exams as she neared the end of her preparation journey. She had completed the steps outlined previously and was at the final stage of practising full written stories which contained all the elements she had learned.

A Walk in the Woods

Crunching through the leaves, Sarah heard a strange noise. She had brown hair and is kind and thoughtful. Sarah froze into a statue. Her greatest fear popped up. A squirrel! She screamed as loud as thunder and ran as fast as a cheetah to the deep, dark, damp woods.

Sarah was kicking leaves and shouting "Hello! Is anyone there?" The echo repeated once, twice and a third time. No-one was there. It was very strange she thought. Lots of creatures lived in the forest. The sun was gone and the only thing that was left was trees. Colossal, black, dull trees. Then Sarah got so bored and wanted to go home. Suddenly, she realised she was lost!

The sun was back but Sarah was lost. Anywhere she went was strange. She didn't know what to do until...a helicopter came! Sarah dashed to get two sticks and she made a fire in the shape of SOS. The helicopter landed and Sarah got in. It took her back to her home. Sarah felt so relieved that she wasn't stuck there forever and ever.

This story would achieve very high marks on a 7+ exam. The student has created:

- an imaginative narrative with a clear beginning in which the character and setting are introduced
- a middle in which tension builds through the use of the senses and a problem is revealed
- an ending in which the problem is resolved and the character reflects on how they feel.

It shows maturity in both vocabulary usage, varied sentence structure and the use of literary techniques such as similes and alliteration. Handwriting, spelling and grammar are all accurate.

Dictation

What is it?

Firstly, it is important to note that not many schools have a dictation section in the assessment. However, as there are a few top schools that do use it, it is important to prepare if your child will be sitting the exam for one of these schools. Do check the requirements for each school. Even if the schools you are applying to don't use dictation on their assessments, it still has value in learning listening skills, grammar, spelling, punctuation and handwriting.

Dictation is the transcription of spoken text: one person who is "dictating" speaks and another who is "taking dictation" writes down the words as they are spoken.

How is it tested?

Dictation tests involve a teacher reading out sentences that your child will need to quickly and accurately write down on paper. The sentence will be read once at normal speed while your child listens, then repeated slower to allow your child to write it down, then repeated at normal speed again allowing your child to check what they wrote.

What are the key skills my child needs to know?

Dictation tests are checking for a number of key skills including:

- listening carefully
- correct spelling
- correct punctuation. Note, the punctuation is not identified by the teacher as they read the sentence (specifically commas, apostrophes, speech marks, question marks and exclamation marks)
- accurate grammar (specifically correct usage of capital letters including for proper nouns)
- understanding correct usage of homophones (their/there/they're, two/to/too)
- clear and neat handwriting

First steps:

Before your child can take part in any dictation exercise, they must already understand all of the age appropriate spellings, punctuation and grammar rules. If your child is still shaky in this area, use commercially produced workbooks to practise these foundation skills first.

Moving on:

Once your child has mastered the spelling, grammar and punctuation rules, you can begin to dictate simple sentences to your child so that they understand how this process works. Use sentences that do not have tricky homophones or complicated grammar at this stage. Remember to read the sentence:

- once at normal speed while your child listens to the sentence and understands it
- a second time slowly, pausing between every 3-4 words while your child writes it down
- a final time at normal speed while your child checks their written work

Next steps:

As your child becomes familiar with how dictation works, you can begin to use longer sentences that contain trickier spellings, punctuation and grammar. At this stage, your child must also get quicker at writing their sentence so it can be completed as you read it out, as well as ensure their handwriting remains neat and clear.

Helpful tips:

- Practise! Dictation improves when it is done regularly.

- Take it in turns. Allow your child to dictate sentences to you to write down and let them check for errors. This is not only fun, but if you make deliberate mistakes, it is a good way for them to learn proof reading!

Example sentences:

The chef hasn't got a kettle.
(Note the contraction and use of apostrophe in 'hasn't' as well as two tricky spelling words)

In July it's hot for the fly in the bottle.
(Note the contraction and use of apostrophe in 'it's' as well as the capital letter for 'July')

"I love apples!" exclaimed the girl as she ran up to the table.
(Note the use of speech marks, the exclamation mark which will be clear in the way the sentence is read out, and the tricky spelling of 'exclaimed')

What is it?

The maths portion of the 7+ exam is a written paper which tests maths knowledge across the entirety of the KS1 curriculum and for some schools dips into the KS2 curriculum. Note that as the exam is taken in the winter of year 2, this means that your child will not have covered all of the curriculum being tested before taking the exam. You will need to ensure to have taught your child these areas yourself.

How is it tested?

The maths paper can take the form of multiple choice questions, but it is much more usual for it to be open answer format, meaning that there are spaces for the students to write the answers. Some schools include a separate mental arithmetic paper, where the questions are read out by the teacher and only the answers are written onto the paper by the children. Calculators are not allowed for the exam.

27

What are the key skills my child needs to know?

Although the entire curriculum must be covered in preparation as questions can be asked on any topic, it is important to note that exams most often have an emphasis on both mental calculations and solving problems.

- **Mental Calculations:** Speed is of the essence here. Solid knowledge of number facts and the ability to work with numbers mentally across all areas of calculation are vital.

- **Problem Solving:** Problem solving is used to assess if your child can *apply* their knowledge. It is a key part of the maths test and is an area in which even the most able children can struggle. Word problems can appear for every area of the maths curriculum. Teaching logical and methodical processes is vital and there is an element of reading comprehension to understanding what is being asked in the questions. Teaching the *vocabulary* of maths is key to understanding the questions.

First steps:

It is important to begin by ensuring your child has a solid understanding of the quantity that a number represents and how it can be manipulated and split up while maintaining that quantity. The focus in this early stage is fun with numbers! You can play different number games with your child, both verbally and with physical objects, to strengthen their understanding that a number is a way of representing a quantity. In addition, your child must memorise number facts such as number bonds to 10, 20 and 100; and 2, 3, 5, 10 times tables.

Moving on:

Once your child has memorised the number facts and demonstrated a solid understating of number, it is time to move on to other areas of the curriculum. Go through the target charts beginning on page 54 and work methodically through each section to identify gaps in knowledge and focus on activities that will help develop these.

Next steps:

When you have ascertained that your child has achieved the maths skills and knowledge identified in the target charts, your child will need to learn how to apply these skills to word problems.

They will not need to learn any new concepts to tackle word problems, but will need to understand how to decode the questions, to identify the maths skill they are being asked to use and how to show their step by step workings in their answer.

In addition, this is the stage in which speed will need to improve on mental and written calculations. Rather than tackling this by using entire practise papers, use commercially produced workbooks for mental arithmetic and encourage your child to get faster on each page.

Helpful hints:

- Memorising number facts can all be done verbally and therefore lends itself to games and locations that are not formal sessions. Counting in multiples, times tables recall and number bonds can all be practised in the car, on walks or even at the dinner table.

- A selection of 12 sided dice can be used for times table games and mental arithmetic practise. They take up very little space in a pocket or bag and can be taken anywhere. The possibilities are endless!

- A4 whiteboards and a set of coloured whiteboard pens make written maths work so much more fun.

- If you are practising a particular maths skill, you will probably be able to find a printable maths game online for it.

- Timers are a fun tool for improving speed. They will encourage your child to work quickly to compete against their previous time. Visual traffic light timers that can be set to specific times are also an exciting alternative.

Examples:

Mental arithmetic:

In this section, there is an expectation that children will work quickly and accurately. 1 mark per question is generally awarded. (Answers are in brackets)

9 + 8 = (17)
28 – 9 = (19)
7 x 3 = (21)
60 ÷ 5 = (12)
102 ÷ 2 = (51)
2410 ÷ 10 = (241)
49 + 27 = (76)
79 – 12 = (67)
97 – 23 = (74)

Sequences:

These questions require your child to work out the pattern of the increase or decrease in the sequence. (Answers are underlined)

26, 29, 33, 38, 44 <u>51</u>
17, 14, 12, 9, 7 <u>4</u>
30, 28, 24, 18, <u>10</u>

Word problems:

These questions require your child to understand the maths that they need to use to solve the problem, and apply their knowledge of maths skills and concepts in a methodical way.

Ravi has 5p. Mickey has 13p. Mary has 42p more than Mickey. If they put their money together, how much do they have?

Answer:

Ravi – 5
Mickey – 13
Mary – 13 + 42 = 55
5 + 13 + 55 = 79p

Fraction questions:

These questions require your child to understand basic fractions of a whole and how to use and understand the correct notation.

Circle the shapes that have exactly one quarter shaded. Write the fraction for the amount shaded in the triangle.

    $\frac{1}{2}$

What is it?

Verbal Reasoning is problem solving based around language and words. Verbal Reasoning reveals how your child takes on board new information by measuring their ability to engage with language. Verbal Reasoning highlights your child's skills in verbal thinking above and beyond their formal literacy abilities. Not all schools test Verbal Reasoning so it is important to check the school's exam process before you begin to prepare your child.

How is it tested?

Verbal Reasoning skills are tested through a variety of question types which can be loosely categorised into the following:

- Word meanings including synonyms, antonyms and links between types of words

- The morphology of words including finding hidden words, creating new words by moving letters, unscrambling words, finding missing letters and alphabetical order

- Identifying patterns in sequences of letters or numbers

35

What are the key skills my child needs to know?

To perform well on verbal reasoning tests, your child needs to have a very strong vocabulary as well as a good grasp of synonyms and antonyms. In addition, solid exam technique will ensure they are able to take their knowledge of words and apply it to the type of question being asked.

The instructions for each type of question can be complex and require your child to read carefully and understand the task. Breaking down the type of questions, understanding the instructions and options for each, and regular practice of each type under *no time pressure* will allow pupils to feel comfortable and confident when they move on to practising full timed tests.

First steps:

If your child has never encountered these types of questions before, begin with a verbal reasoning workbook that is aimed at children at least a year younger than your child. The early books aimed at ages 5-6 are much easier to understand and generally quite fun. Sit with your child for the first few sessions and help explain each type of question to them. For the answer they chose, have them explain *why* they chose it.

Moving on:

Once your child is familiar with the types of questions, they can work through the exercises on their own. Check and score each one they do, so that you can see if there are any question types they are struggling with. Do not worry about speed at this stage. Allow them as long as they need and encourage them to be accurate. There are multiple publishers for these practise books so your child will have plenty of opportunity to work on specific question types for longer if they are struggling before you move on to the next steps.

Next steps:

When your child is working through books at the right level for their age, or even slightly ahead (books aged at 7-8 years old should be the level they reach in the couple of months before the exams), you can begin to work on speed. Set a timer and encourage them to work to the time given but still remain accurate.

Helpful hints:

- Play verbal word games. Say a word and ask your child to tell you a synonym or antonym.

- Use scrabble tiles or other letter tiles to practise understanding the morphology of words. Give your child 3 or 4 letters and ask them to make as many words as they can from them.

- Use scrabble tiles or other letter tiles to give your child a word. Challenge them to change only one letter tile to make a new word.

- Play alphabet games. Call out two words and ask which comes first alphabetically.

- Use word cards to practise alphabetical order. Use two piles of cards and see who can put them in order in the fastest time.

- Crosswords aimed at young children are fun and help improve understanding of the morphology of words.

Example questions:

Word meanings:

1. Underline the two words, one from each group, that are closest in meaning.

    (<u>dog</u>, sheep, cow) (cat, horse, <u>hound</u>)

2. Complete the following sentences by selecting the most sensible word from each group of words given in the brackets. Underline the words selected.

    The (<u>moon</u>, sun, clouds) was very (dark, rainy, <u>bright</u>) in the night (wind, sun, <u>sky</u>)

3. Underline the word that has the most similar meaning to the word in capital letters

    JOYFUL   unhappy <u>cheerful</u> frown sparkling

4. Underline the two words, one from each group, that together make a new word.

    Example: (<u>basket</u>, bag, shop) (pin, <u>ball</u>, bin)

Morphology of words:

1. Change one letter at a time to make the first word into the final word

   WAS (____WAN_____) FAN

2. Find the four letter word hidden at the end of one word and the beginning of another.

   Sam used his ink to draw the picture of the sky.

3. Rearrange the jumbled letter to create a sensible word that fits the sentence.

   Saul played BOLAOLFT (FOOTBALL) in the garden.

Patterns and sequences:

1. Use the number code for the word you are given to answer the questions.

    If the code for TEACH is 57341:

    What is 435 the code for? _____ (CAT)

2. Use the alphabet to help you fill in the missing numbers and letters.

    A B C D E F G H I J K L M N O P Q R S T
    U V W X Y Z

    PN is to MK as WU is to _____ (TR)

What is it?

Non-verbal reasoning is a test of problem solving based around pictures and diagrams. It is designed to see how your child can use critical thinking and logic to solve problems. It is considered a good indication of your child's mathematical capabilities and powers of deduction. It does not test learned ability but becoming familiar with the types of questions being used on these tests is an advantage. The vast majority of schools test non-verbal reasoning on the 7+ exam.

How is it tested?

Non-verbal reasoning skills are tested through a variety of question types which can be loosely categorised into the following types:

- Finding patterns in shapes including shading, size, proportion, direction and position

- Identifying similarities and differences in shapes including symmetry, reflection and rotation

- Solving sequences and matrices using numbers, shapes, position and directions

43

What are the key skills my child needs to know?

As with verbal reasoning, familiarity with question types and regular practise will help improve scores. An excellent technique for teaching non-verbal reasoning is to ask your child to verbalise the rule or reasoning for the question they are answering and get them to apply it to each possible answer.

For visual learners, drawing shapes and reflections on paper can also aid practice. As with verbal reasoning, take the time pressure off during the learning phase and only do timed tests once you are sure your child has a solid understanding of all the question types and can answer them with ease.

First steps:

If your child has never encountered these types of questions before, begin with a non-verbal reasoning workbook that is aimed at children at least a year younger than your child is. The early books aimed at ages 5-6 are much easier to understand and generally quite fun. Sit with your child for the first few sessions and help explain each type of question to them. For the answer they chose, have them explain *why* they chose it.

Once your child is familiar with the type of questions, they can work through the exercises on their own. Check and score each one they do, so that you can see if there are any question types they are struggling with. Do not worry about speed at this stage. Allow them as long as they need and encourage them to be accurate.

Next steps:

When your child is working through books at the right level for their age, or even slightly ahead (books aged at 7-8 years old should be the level they reach in the couple of months before the exams), you can begin to work on speed. Set a timer and encourage them to work to the time given but still remain accurate.

Helpful hints:
- Use a hand held mirror to explore reflections. Discuss what you can see in the mirror and how an object changes.
- Use real objects to think about rotation. You can also cut out 2D shapes from cardboard and lay them flat on a table to explore rotation.
- Explore extending patterns by making simple flashcards. Print some patterns from a non-verbal reasoning workbook. Cut out the shapes and lay them on a table to make patterns.

Example questions:

Which of these pictures is the odd one out? Circle the letter.

A   B   C   (D)   E

This question type requires your child to notice similarities and differences between the pictures. In this case, the direction of arrow D is anticlockwise whereas all the other arrows are pointing in a clockwise direction.

Which picture on the right belongs to the group on the left? Circle the letter.

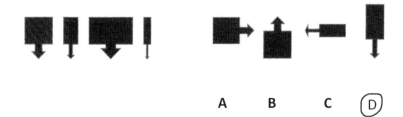

A   B   C   (D)

This question requires your child to identify a feature that is common for all the shapes on the left and choose the shape on the right that fits with this common feature. In this case, all of the shapes on the left have an arrow that points downwards. Shape D is the only one on the right that shares this feature.

Which picture on the right goes in the empty space?

A B C D

This question type requires your child to identify repeating patterns. They must look carefully at more than one feature of the shapes, recognise the pattern, and determine which shape comes next. In this case, the triangle and internal oval remain the same position but their colours alternate between black and white.

Pretend the vertical line is a mirror. Which picture on the right is a reflection of the picture on the left?

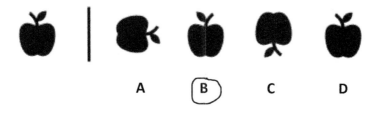

A B C D

This question type requires your child to understand that when a shape is reflected, it maintains the same size and angles but is just reversed.

Once your child has developed the skills in each element of the exam and you have ticked "achieved" on each target, you will need to begin to think about exam techniques that will help ensure that your child performs on the exam to the best of their ability. For each area, I have listed the key techniques that you should focus on.

Reading comprehension:

- Read *all* of the text! Children often ignore titles, subheadings and information after the text about the author. If these are printed on the page, then they are important!

- Focus. Speed is important in reading but not if the words are just read mechanically without meaning. Focusing attention on the content as it is being read is essential.

- Read each question carefully and underline key words in the question.

- Scan and skim the text. There is not time to re-read the entire text to find the answer. Your child must become proficient at scanning and skimming for key words to pin point the area of the text where the answer may be.

- Once pin pointed, re-read that portion of the text carefully. Children often fall into the trap of skimming for key words and jumping right to answering the question thereby missing pertinent information.

- Never rely on memory! Your child must check for the answer in the text regardless of whether they think they remember the information.

- Knowledge of figurative language types as well as word classes is important as questions may ask your child to find an example of such in the text.

- Unless it explicitly says so in the question (i.e. *Imagine* what….), the answers do not come from your child's imagination and evidence should always be found in the text.

50

Writing composition:

- Plan! Teaching your child to take the time to plan their writing is vital. The form this planning takes will depend on the task given and the time scales allowed. However, even basic 2 minutes "in the head" planning of beginning, middle and end will make a significant difference to coherent writing. Some schools give both space and time for planning at the beginning of the composition task and your child should understand how to use this if they encounter this as part of the task.

- Show off! The only piece of writing the school will see from your child is this task. Therefore, it is imperative that your child uses their "best" vocabulary and imaginative ideas to show what they are capable of.

- Quality over quantity! There is a limit to how much can be written within the time scales given (which will vary widely). It is much more important to write less, but with skill and sophistication, than to try to cover reams of paper.

- Check it over! Your child must learn to leave time at the end to check their work. Spelling and grammar are being tested as part of the writing composition tasks and every mistake that is corrected is worth the time taken.

Maths:

- Timing is key. Your child should move speedily through the mental calculations section. If stuck, move on and come back later if there is time.

- Understand the points for each question. Is it worth taking 5 minutes over a 1 point question?

- Show workings on word problems! When a question is worth more than one point, this is sometimes because there will be partial points available for the workings.

- Pay attention to any example questions/solutions given.

- Understand that some questions may well go beyond what your child has been taught and are designed to challenge them and assess how they approach the problem. These should only be attempted if time remains, but should be attempted even if your child is unsure about how to proceed.

Reasoning:

- Read the instructions for each question type carefully and look at the example given. Your child should not assume that because they have done similar questions in practise, the instructions will be exactly the same.

- Be methodical. Your child should look at all of the possible answers and work through them one by one. They can cross out any that are definitely incorrect.

- Don't leave any questions blank. If your child needs to skip a question, they can come back to it at the end of the test and try again. It is better to circle an answer than leave it totally blank.

- Work quickly but accurately.

Keeping Track of Progress

The charts on the following pages will help you to keep track of your child's progress, and focus on the key skills needed to be successful in the exam. At regular intervals, you should refer to these charts and think about how your child is progressing.

Working towards: Your child is learning this skill but has not yet become reliably proficient. They need more practice and time to fully understand and demonstrate this objective.

Achieved: Your child has reached this target and regularly shows you their attainment in activities that they do.

Exam Ready: Your child is able to consistently achieve high marks on this target on practise papers within the time scales set.

Reading Comprehension

Target	Working Towards	Achieved	Exam Ready
Read with fluency including most common words by sight			
Explain and discuss their understanding of the text			
Explain the meaning of words in context			
Draw inferences about the text			
Predict what might happen next			
Identify how language, structure and presentation contribute to meaning e.g. that the use of the word 'trembling' indicates that the kitten is scared			
Answer the question in a full sentence using appropriate structure			

Writing Composition

Target	Working Towards	Achieved	Exam Ready
Interesting and imaginative ideas that relate to the story prompt			
A clear beginning, middle and end structured in paragraphs			
Use of ideas to develop tension and/or emotion in the middle paragraph			
Interesting use of mature and varied vocabulary			
Use of figurative language			
Use of a variety of sentence openers			
Mix of simple and complex sentences			
Consistent use of verb tenses			
Consistent use of either 1st person or 3rd person narration			
Correct use of punctuation			
Accurate spelling			
Neat cursive handwriting			
Can write within the given time scale			

Maths

Target	Working Towards	Achieved	Exam Ready
Counting, properties of numbers, number sequences			
Describe and extend simple number sequences: count on or back in steps of 1, 2, 3, 4, 5 or 10, starting from any two-digit number			
Count in hundreds from and back to zero			
Recognise odd and even numbers			
Recognise two-digit multiples of 2, 5 or 10			
Place value and ordering			
Know what each digit in a two-digit number represents, including 0 as a place holder and partition two-digit numbers into a multiple of ten and ones			
Compare two given two-digit numbers, say which is more or less and give a number which lies between them			
Position up to any three-digit number on a number line			

Estimating and rounding			
Use the vocabulary of estimation and approximation			
Round any two-digit number to the nearest 10			
Fractions			
Recognise and find one half and one quarter of shapes and small numbers of objects			
Recognise that two halves or four quarters make one whole and that two quarters and one half are equivalent			
Addition and subtraction			
Understand the operations of addition and subtraction and use the related vocabulary			
Multiplication and division			
Understand that subtraction is the inverse of addition			
Recognise that addition can be done in any order, but not subtraction			
Add three single-digit numbers mentally			
Add two two-digit numbers with any appropriate method			
Know by heart all addition facts to a total of 20 and the corresponding subtraction facts			

Know by heart all pairs of multiples of 10 with a total of 100			
Derive quickly TU + U up to a total of 50 and the corresponding subtractions.			
Understand the operation of multiplication as repeated addition			
Understand division as grouping (repeated subtraction) or sharing			
Know and use halving as the inverse of doubling			
Know by heart multiplication facts for the 2, 3, 5 and 10 times-tables			
Know by heart doubles of all numbers to 10 and the corresponding halves			
Derive quickly division facts corresponding to the 2, 5 and 10 times tables - doubles of all numbers to 15.			
Derive quickly doubles of multiples of 5 to 50			
Derive quickly halves of multiples of 10 to 100 (e.g. half of 70)			

Money and measures			
Recognise all coins and use £.p notation for money			
Find totals, give change and work out which coins to pay			
Use mental addition and subtraction, simple multiplication and division, to solve simple word problems involving numbers in money and measures, using one or two steps			
Use the vocabulary related to length			
Read a simple scale to the nearest labelled division, including using a ruler to draw and measure lines to the nearest centimetre			
Use and read the vocabulary related to time			
Use units of time and know the relationships between them (minute, hour, day, week)			
Read the time to the hour, half hour or quarter hour on an analogue clock and a 12-hour digital clock and understand the notation 7:30			

Geometry			
Use everyday language to describe features of familiar 2-D shapes, including circle, triangle, square and rectangle, referring to properties such as the number of sides			
Sort shapes and describe some of their features, such as the number of sides and corners, symmetry (2-D shapes)			
Know the properties and names of common 3D shapes			
Recognise line symmetry			
Use mathematical vocabulary to describe position, direction and movement: for example, describe, place, tick, draw or visualise objects in given positions			
Recognise whole, half and quarter turns, to the left or right, clockwise or anti-clockwise			
Solving problems			
Choose and use appropriate operations of up to 2 steps to solve word problems and appropriate ways of calculating			

66

Verbal Reasoning

Target	Working Towards	Achieved	Exam Ready
Identify words with similar meanings			
Identify words with opposite meanings			
Find common links between words in a group			
Identifying word meanings			
Understand the morphology of words – finding hidden words			
Understanding the morphology of words – creating words by moving letters			
Understand and use alphabetical order			
Identify the link between pairs of letters in order to find the missing letter			

Non-Verbal Reasoning

Target	Working Towards	Achieved	Exam Ready
Identify similarities in shapes for grouping			
Find patterns in shapes including shading, size and proportion			
Find patterns where the position of elements change or show direction			
Identify images that have lines of symmetry, reflection or rotation			
Solve sequences using numbers, shapes, position or directions			
Solve matrices questions using shapes			

Staying Positive

Pressure to succeed on entrance exams is an issue for you and your child. The impact of this pressure cannot be underestimated and can have a very real effect on learning. Even if you feel that you are hiding your stress from your child, they are very likely to be picking up on it. Staying positive throughout the process is key. If you are worried that your child is beginning to feel the pressure, look out for the following signs:

- Mood changes, such as being tearful, angry or withdrawn.

- Not wanting to go to school or to come and do a preparation session when they have previously been fine.

- Complaining of stomach aches, headaches, or other physical symptoms that are not attributable to a physical illness.

- Changes in their sleeping or eating habits.

- Low self-esteem, such as calling themselves 'stupid' or saying they're 'rubbish'.

- Reacting extremely if they make mistakes in their work

What makes a difference to stress levels for both you and your child:

- Feeling supported rather than pressured by those around them. For you, talk to others going through the same process. Share ideas and concerns. For your child, make sure they feel that you are on their side.

- A sense of control over their learning. Give your child choices. While there is no escaping the need to get the preparation done, they might be able to choose which activity they want to do that day.

- A positive outlook – help your child to have fun and laugh as well as learn

- Feeling prepared. If you follow the steps and keep track of progress, you will feel more prepared for each part of the process. Letting your child know what is coming each day will also help them feel more prepared.

How to help:

- Listen to and acknowledge your child's feelings. Help them understand that it is OK to feel worried about the exams and not want to do extra work.

- Show them how far they have come and emphasise the positive. Highlight their strengths. It is a great idea to keep examples of work from the beginning of the journey (such as a story they wrote) and remind them how they have improved.

- Don't overload them with extra work and ensure they get plenty of breaks at weekends. Small amounts of regular work is much more manageable than trying to fit in long and arduous sessions all in one go at the weekend.

- Don't forget the importance of exercise and sleep!

Congratulations! If you have got to this page, it means your child has been called back for the second stage assessment process and the work you have put into preparing them has all been worthwhile.

Many parents and children find this stage of the journey very daunting. The word "interview" strikes fear into many adults. However, rest assured that an assessment day is nothing that should induce panic. Every school will go out of their way to ensure that both you and your child feel relaxed and welcome.

What is it?

An assessment day is the second stage of the entrance exam process. Generally, approximately two children per place available will be invited to the school with their parents. Children will spend time in a classroom with a group of other prospective students and a teacher. Children will take part in a variety of activities designed to further assess their English and Maths skills as well as skills, such as listening and working with others.

How is it tested?

Every school will design their assessment day differently. However, you can expect that your child might be asked to:

- do some writing
- read aloud and answer comprehension questions verbally about what they have read
- take part in a mental maths activity (either singly or as part of a group)
- participate in a group activity designed to assess if they can follow instructions and collaborate with others.

As part of the session, it is not unusual for children to be asked some interview style questions by the Head Teacher and a Class Teacher.

What are the key skills my child needs to know?

Your child will need to feel confident about speaking to unfamiliar adults and other children. They will need to be prepared to answer questions about themselves with more detail than a one or two word response. It is helpful if they can show a genuine desire and interest to attend the school to which they are applying. They should remain practised in the key areas of English and Maths as these are likely to be part of the assessment day.

Helpful hints:

It is very important to understand that you cannot fully prepare your child for an interview and assessment day. Drilling them on prepared questions and answers will be completely counter-productive to them displaying their true selves on the day.

However, there are plenty of activities you can do that will ensure they are confident and comfortable when they attend the assessment.

- Provide plenty of opportunities for your child to talk about their day, their interests and books they are reading. Encourage them to continue and expand on their thoughts if they stop short but remember that an answer is never "wrong". All of their thoughts and interests are valid!

- Talk to your child about the school where they are sitting the assessment. Discuss together all of the activities they are excited to do, once they attend. Your child should genuinely feel enthusiasm about this new adventure!

- Body language and clarity of speech is important. If your child speaks very softly, try to encourage them to speak up. Keeping long hair tied back so that it does not act as a tempting fidget object is advisable.

Recommended Reading List

Banks, Lynne Reid	Harry and the Poisonous Centipede
Bond, Michael	Paddington series
Brown, Jeff	The Flat Stanley series
Cresswell, Helen	The Secret World of Polly Flint
Dahl, Roald	The Twits
Dahl, Roald	George's Marvellous Medicine
Dahl, Roald	The Magic Finger
Dahl, Roald	The Giraffe and the Pelly and Me
Fitzhugh, Louise	Harriet the Spy
Grahame, Kenneth	The Reluctant Dragon
Ingalls Wilder, Laura	Little House in the Big Woods
Juster, Norton	The Phantom Tolbooth
Kastner, Erich	Emil and the Detectives
King, Clive	Stig of the Dump
King Smith, Dick	The Sheep Pig
Morpurgo, Michael	The Butterfly Lion
Morpurgo, Michael	The Dancing Bear
Murphy, Jill	The Worst Witch
Norton, Mary	The Borrowers
Pearce, Phillipa	The Battle of Bubble and Squeak
Pope Osborne, Mary	Magic Tree House series
Tomlinson, Jill	The Owl Who Was Afraid of the Dark
White, E.B.	Charlotte's Web
Whybrow, Ian	Little Wolf series

Further Information and Guidance

The process of preparing your child for the 7+ exams can sometimes feel overwhelming. I have confidence that by following this handbook and putting in regular practice, your child will make improvements.

However, if you feel that you need further resources or guidance, you can find a variety of solutions such as tuition, assessments and consultations at:

www.educationpathfinder.co.uk

7+ English
Practice Exam 1
(60 minutes)

Instructions:

Part A Comprehension: You have 30 minutes to
                            read the passage and
                            answer the questions. This
                            section is worth 25 marks

Part B Composition: You have 35 minutes to
                            write your story. This
                            section is worth 25 points.

Work as quickly as you can.

Name:

_____

Part A Comprehension (24 marks): 30 minutes.

Read the passage and then answer the following questions in full sentences.

All of a sudden Peter leaped to his feet and ran hastily after the goats. Heidi followed him as fast as she could, for she was too eager to know what had happened to stay behind. Peter dashed through the middle of the flock towards that side of the mountain where the rocks fell perpendicularly to a great depth below and where any thoughtless goat, if it went too near, might fall over and break all its legs. He had caught sight of the <u>inquisitive</u> Greenfinch taking leaps in that direction and he was only just in time, for the animal had already sprung to the edge of the abyss. All Peter could do was to throw himself down and seize one of her hind legs. Greenfinch, thus taken by surprise, began bleating furiously, angry at being held so fast and prevented from continuing her voyage of discovery. She struggled to get loose and endeavoured so obstinately to leap forward that Peter shouted to Heidi to come and help him, for he could not get up and was afraid of pulling out the goat's leg altogether.

Heidi had already run up and she saw at once the danger both Peter and the animal were in. She quickly <u>gathered</u> a bunch of sweet-smelling leave and then, holding them under Greenfinch's nose, said coaxingly, "Come, come, Greenfinch, you must not be naughty! Look, you might fall down there and break your leg and that would give you dreadful pain!"

The young animal turned quickly and began contentedly eating the leaves out of Heidi's hand. Meanwhile Peter got on to his feet again and took hold of Greenfinch by the band round her neck from which her bell was hung and Heidi, taking hold of her in the same way on the other side, they led the wanderer back to the rest of the flock that had remained peacefully feeding. Peter, now he had his goat in safety, lifted his stick in order to give her a good beating as punishment, and Greenfinch seeing what was coming shrank back in fear. But Heidi cried out, "No, no, Peter, you must not strike her; see how frightened she is!"

"She deserves it," growled Peter and again lifted his stick. Then Heidi flung herself against him and cried indignantly, "You have no right to touch her, it will hurt her, let her alone!"

Peter looked with surprise at the commanding little figure, whose dark eyes were flashing, and reluctantly, he let his stick drop. "Well, I will let her off if you will give me some more of your cheese tomorrow," he said, for he was determined to have something to make up to him for his fright.

"You shall have it all, tomorrow and every day, I do not want it," replied Heidi, giving ready consent to his demand. "And I will give you bread as well, a large piece like you had today; but then you must promise never to beat Greenfinch, or Snowflake, or any of the goats."

"All right," said Peter, "I don't care," which meant that he would agree to the bargain and let go of Greenfinch, who joyfully sprang to join her companions.

Taken from "Heidi" by Johanna Spygri

Now answer the following questions:

1. Why did Heidi follow Peter when he ran after the goats? (1 mark)

_____

_____

2. Why did Peter throw himself down and seize hold of the goat's hind legs? (1 mark)

_____

_____

3. Tick two boxes next to the words that best describe how Peter felt when he called for Heidi's help. (2 marks)

☐ worried   ☐ shy   ☐ angry

☐ fed up   ☐ sad   ☐ excited

☐ hopeful   ☐ scared

4. a) Why did Heidi hold sweet smelling leaves under the Greenfinch's nose? (2 marks)

_____

_____

_____

_____

5. (a) Why did Peter lift his stick to the goat? (1 mark)

_____

_____

(b) How did the goat react? (1 mark)

_____

_____

_____

6. Why do you think Peter said, "Well, I will let her off if you will give me some more of your cheese tomorrow"? (3 marks)

_____

_____

_____

_____

7. What sort of person do you think Heidi was? (3 marks)

_____

_____

_____

_____

8. Find a synonym or meaning for the following words <u>as they are used in the context of the story.</u> They are underlined for you in the passage. (4 marks)

(a) inquisitive:

_____

_____

(b) gathered:

_____

_____

(c) reluctantly:

_____

_____

(d) companions:

_____

_____

9. <u>Underline and correct</u> the mistakes in the sentence below. There are four to find. (2 marks)

peter huried to grab the Greenfinches leg and pull him back

_____

_____

10. Circle the correct word: (4 marks)

    a. Circle an adjective:
       little   threw   tea   goat

    b. Circle a connective:
       large   rock   anyone   and

    c. Circle an adverb:
       jumped   wildly   hat   his

    d. Circle a pronoun:
       funny   coughed   her   large

Part B Composition (25 marks):

Write a story called: <u>My Lost Animal</u> about your own animal that has gone on an adventure. Remember to include lots of interesting details and vocabulary and to check your spelling and punctuation.

_____

_____

_____

_____

_____

_____

_____

_____

_____

_____

_____

_____

_____

Sample Answers
Paper 1

Comprehension:

These are sample answers. Variations on these answers may still be acceptable and gain the marks.

1. Heidi followed Peter because she was eager to know what had happened.
2. Peter threw himself down and seized the goat's hind leg because he was trying to stop it from falling over the edge of the mountain.
3. Worried, scared
4. Heidi held the sweet smelling leaves under the Greenfinch's nose to coax it back from the mountain edge.
5.
   a. Peter lifted his stick to the goat because he was angry and wanted to punish it.
   b. The goat shrank back in fear.
6. Peter said this because he wanted something to make up for the fright he had had and he was also surprised that he had followed Heidi's command.
7. Heidi is a kind and caring person. She stopped Peter from hurting the goat and also gave up her food to keep the goat safe.
8.
   a. Curious
   b. Collect
   c. Unwillingly
   d. Friends

9. Peter hurried to grab the Greenfinch's leg and pull him back.
10.
    a. little
    b. and
    c. wildly
    d. her

Composition:

Composition marking is subjective. However, marks are awarded in the following general categories:

Ideas and story structure: 10 marks
(Stories should be imaginative while not straying from the topic given. They should have a clear beginning, middle and end and use paragraphs.)
Spelling and punctuation: 6 marks
(Spelling should be accurate and punctuation should be used correctly throughout.)
Use of varied and interesting vocabulary: 6 marks
(Vocabulary should be varied, expressive and include interesting adjectives and powerful verbs.)
Presentation (handwriting):   3 marks
(Handwriting should be clear and presentable.)

7+ Maths
Practice Exam 1
(45 minutes)

Instructions:

You have 45 minutes. This section is worth 25 points.

Work as quickly as you can. Show your workings.

Name:

_____

Work out the following sums:

1) $5 + 8 =$ ☐

2) $28 - 9 =$ ☐

3) $17 + 28 =$ ☐

4) $60 \div 5 =$ ☐

5) $97 - 23 =$ ☐

Fill in the missing number:

6) ____ $+ 9 = 37$

7) ____ $- 9 = 20$

8) ____ $\div 4 = 6$

9) $49 =$ ____ $+ 13 + 21$

10) $16 +$ ____ $= 50 - 10$

11) Circle two numbers that add up to 82:

27   51   12   27   60   15   9
            22   4   61

Solve the following problems:

12) Sarah has 12 pencils and Ben has 24 pencils.
How many pencils do they have altogether?

13) Poppy has 9 fewer sweets than Karis. If Karis has
51 sweets, how many sweets does Poppy have?

14) A packet of crisps costs 7 pence. How much
would it cost in total to buy a packet of crisps
everyday for a whole week?

15) Debra has £64 but she spends half in a shop.
How much does she have left?

16) Mum had to make cookies for a bake sale. She could fit 3 cookies on each tray. How many trays does she need for 27 cookies?

17) Put these numbers in order from the largest to the smallest:

23   15   99   60   45   88   62   90

_____

Complete the following sequences:

18) 26, 29, 33, 38, 44, _____

19) 50, 39, 28, _____, 6

20) 900ml, 700ml, 500ml, _____

Answer the following questions:

21) Sam goes to bed at 7:30pm. His brother Ted
    goes to bed one hour later. Draw the hands on
    the clock to show what time Ted goes to bed.

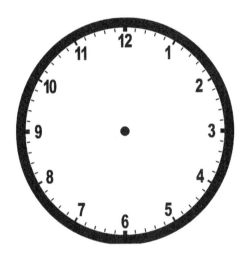

22) What fraction of the circle below has a shape in
    it? _____

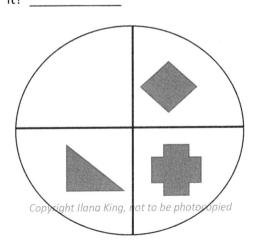

99

Round these numbers to the nearest 10:

23) 49 _____

24) 81 _____

25) 5 _____

26) 99 _____

27. Fill in the missing numbers. All of the
    numbers in a straight line follow the
    same rule:

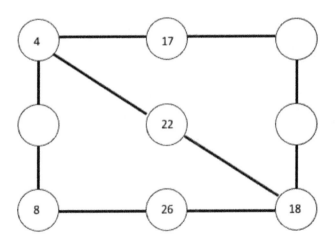

Answers
Paper 1

1. 13
2. 19
3. 45
4. 12
5. 74
6. 28
7. 29
8. 24
9. 15
10. 24
11. 60, 22
12. 36
13. 42
14. 49p
15. £32
16. 9
17. 99, 90, 88, 62, 60, 45, 23, 15
18. 51
19. 17
20. 300ml
21.

22. ¾
23. 50
24. 80
25. 10
26. 100

27.

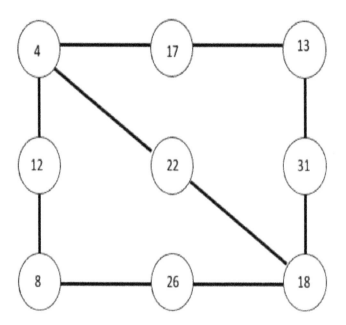

7+ Reasoning
Practice Exam 1
(30 minutes)

Instructions:

You have 30 minutes. This section is worth 46 points.

Work as quickly as you can.

Name:

_____

Underline the two words, one from each group, that are closest in meaning.

Example: (<u>dog</u>, sheep, cow)   (cat, horse, <u>hound</u>)

1) (sky, earth, grass)   (ground, star, cloud)

2) (table, chair, couch)   (sofa, rug, stool)

3) (happy, tired, angry)   (excited, cheerful, sad)

4) (false, fear, fun)   (unhappy, untrue, uneven)

Change one letter at a time to make the first word into the final word

Example: WAS   (____WAN____)
FAN

5) CAR   _____   HAT

6) FOG   _____   DOT

7) TWO   _____   BOO

8) BIN   _____   FIT

Find the four letter word hidden at the end of one word and the beginning of another.

Example: Sam used hi<u>s ink</u> to draw the picture of the sky.

9) I saw the yellow sun.

10) The bed had pillows and a sheet.

11) I had to stop laying down on the floor.

12) Help me attempt this problem!

Rearrange the jumbled letter to create a sensible word that fits the sentence.

Example: Saul played BOLAOLFT in the garden.
_____FOOTBALL_____

13) The LLUMBERA kept her dry.

_____

14) Choose your book in the YBRRILA

_____

15) It's a beautiful day to ride my CCYLEBI

_____

Complete the sentences by underlining the correct word in brackets.

Example: Car is to land as boat is to (river, <u>water</u>, sky)

16) Fork is to knife as cup is to (saucer, plate, jug)

17) Cow is to calf as horse is to (kid, piglet, foal)

18) Glass is to window as brick is to (door, wall, roof)

Use the alphabet to help you fill in the missing numbers and letters.

A B C D E F G H I J K L M N O P Q R S T U V W X Y Z

EXAMPLE: PN is to MK as WU is to _____TR)___

19) DE is to IJ as MN is to _____

20) TO is to MH as RM is to _____

21) FE is to IH as RQ is to _____

Use the number code for the word you are given to answer the questions.

Example: If the code for TEACH is 57341:

    What is 435 the code for? ___CAT___

If the code for BADGER is 835469

    22) What is the code for RAGE _____?

    23) What is 8639 the code for _____?

    24) What is the code for BEAD_____?

Underline the two words, one from each group, that together make a new word.

Example: (<u>basket</u>, bag, shop) (pin, <u>ball</u>, bin)

    25) (super, great, flower) (ball, market, shop)

    26) (heat, fire, flame)   (fighter, hero, girl)

    27) (note, pen, paper) (magazine, book, newspaper)

    28) (sky, moon, sun)   (tree, flower, shrub)

Which of these pictures is the odd one out? Circle the letter.

Example:

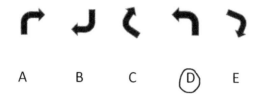

A   B   C   (D)   E

29)

A   B   C   D   E

30)

A   B   C   D   E

31)

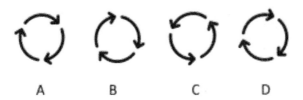

A   B   C   D

Which picture on the right belongs with the picture on the left? Circle the letter.

Example:

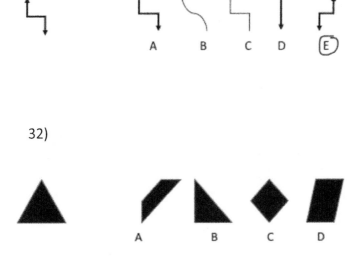

A   B   C   D   E

32)

A   B   C   D

33)

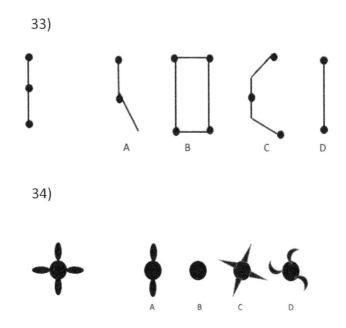

A   B   C   D

34)

A   B   C   D

Pretend the vertical line is a mirror. Which picture on the right is a reflection of the picture on the left?

Example:

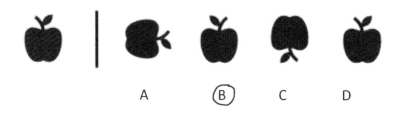

A   B   C   D

35)

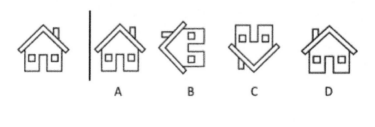

36)

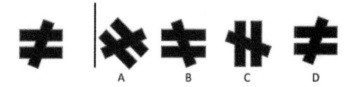

37)

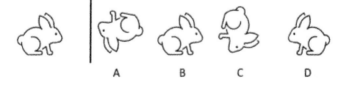

Which of the pictures on the right best fits into the space in the grid?

Example:

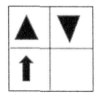 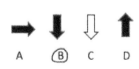

38)

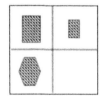 

39)

40)

A   B   C   D

The first two pictures go together. Which of the five pictures on the right goes with the third picture in some way?

Example:

A   B   C   D

41)

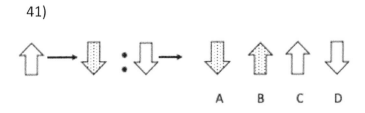

A   B   C   D

42)

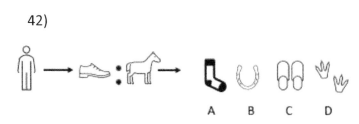

A   B   C   D

43)

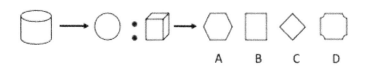

A   B   C   D

Which picture on the right goes in the empty space?

Example:

A   B   C

D

44)

45)

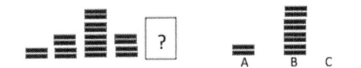

46)

Answers
Paper 1

1) earth, ground
2) couch, sofa
3) happy, cheerful
4) false, untrue
5) CAT
6) DOG
7) TOO
8) FIN
9) they
10) sand
11) play
12) meat
13) umbrella
14) library
15) bicycle
16) saucer
17) foal
18) wall
19) RS
20) KF
21) UT
22) 9346
23) BEAR
24) 8635
25) supermarket
26) firefighter
27) notebook
28) sunflower
29) E
30) D

31) C
32) B
33) C
34) C
35) D
36) B
37) D
38) C
39) D
40) B
41) B
42) B
43) B
44) D

Printed in Great Britain
by Amazon